Summary: For a child, the time between sundown and sunup can be
an enchanting world of mystery and fun, a time when fairies dance,
night creatures creak and hum, and stars reign over all. What are a
child's thoughts when he or she hears the evening's first cricket, has a
sleepover with friends, or looks up at the stars and wonders, "What's
up there?"

Clear Fork Publishing
P.O. Box 870
102 S. Swenson
Stamford, Texas 79553
(325)773-5550
www.clearforkpublishing.com

Printed and Bound in the United States of America.

ISBN - 978-1-946101-31-0
LCN - 2017946100

Dean, to our shared moon of midnights over the years.
Maris & Jake, shimmer! - Raven

To Sergio, who empowers me.
To Susana, who knows my heart.
and to those few other souls which are always by my side and are part of my heart as well. - Carina

In Outer Space

Looking through
My telescope
Space doesn't seem so far;
Glowing above our neighborhood-
A crescent moon
And stars.

If somebody in space looked back
I wonder what they'd see...
Would they spy my telescope?
Would they notice me?

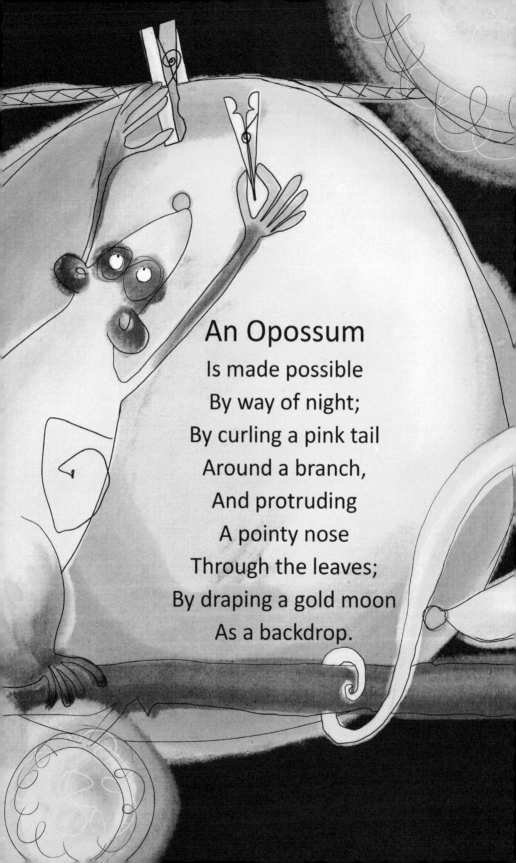

An Opossum

Is made possible
By way of night;
By curling a pink tail
Around a branch,
And protruding
A pointy nose
Through the leaves;
By draping a gold moon
As a backdrop.

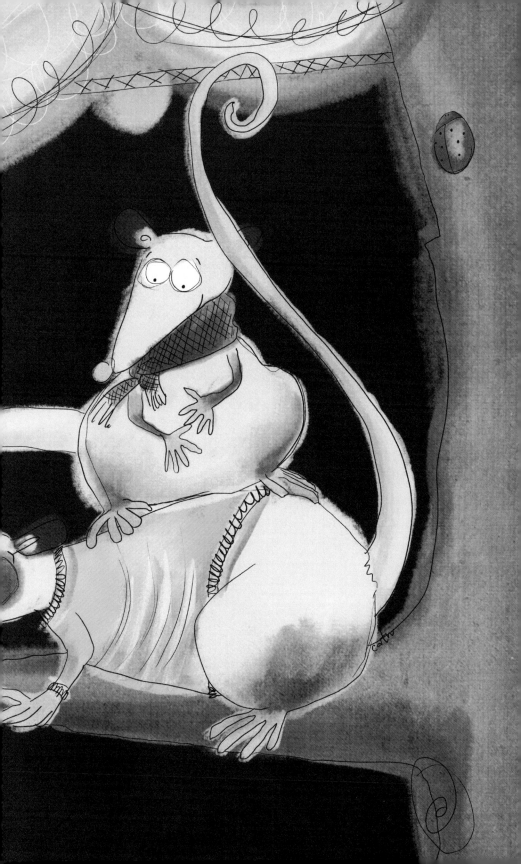

A Sweet Night

I press my nose
Against the screen
And squint into the night.
The dusk's as thick
As chocolate cake -
I'd like to take a bite!

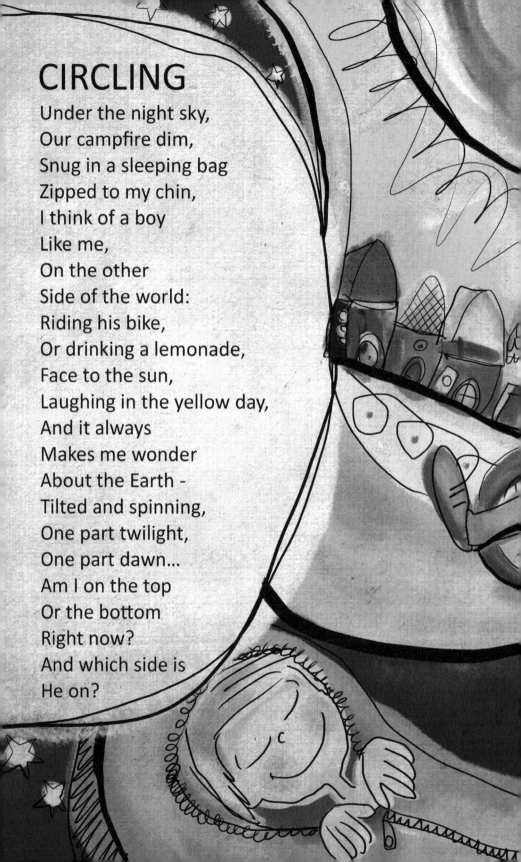

CIRCLING

Under the night sky,
Our campfire dim,
Snug in a sleeping bag
Zipped to my chin,
I think of a boy
Like me,
On the other
Side of the world:
Riding his bike,
Or drinking a lemonade,
Face to the sun,
Laughing in the yellow day,
And it always
Makes me wonder
About the Earth -
Tilted and spinning,
One part twilight,
One part dawn...
Am I on the top
Or the bottom
Right now?
And which side is
He on?

Sonata

Hummmm...
Hummmm...
Night comes,
Earth strums
Its silver string,
Casting shadows
To the wind.
The night bird
And the cricket
Tune their flute
And violin.

I blink my heavy eyes,
Rest my hand under my chin
And smile
When the bullfrog joins in.

A Shooting Star

From the corner of my eye
I see a star streaking the sky,
Dashing from the moon's front yard-
A runaway, a shooting shard,
Zipping quickly toward uptown,
Sprinting, racing, falling down.

Perhaps it only wants to know
What all the lights are here below,
But absent from it's cosmic place-
Is there a hole now
Up in space?

If Night Could Talk

It would say
Hush.
It would say
Quiet down,
Slow down,
Share the secrets of the day
With me.
It would rustle
And whisper,
Wrap its sparkling
Velvet cloak
Across the sky,
Sigh

And murmur
Good night.

Hide and Seek

I skitter, I flitter
I leap and pounce.
I reach, I stretch,
And spring, and bounce.

In hide and seek -
It's here, then gone,
This firefly
Upon our lawn.

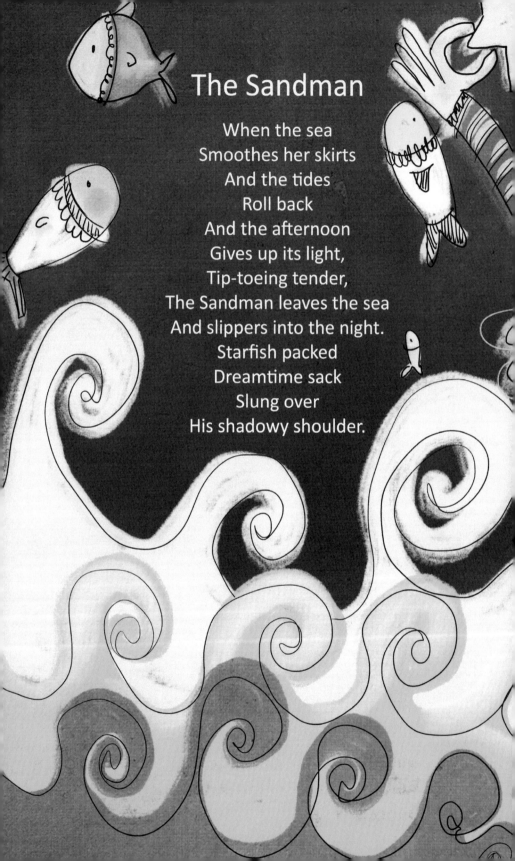

The Sandman

When the sea
Smoothes her skirts
And the tides
Roll back
And the afternoon
Gives up its light,
Tip-toeing tender,
The Sandman leaves the sea
And slippers into the night.
Starfish packed
Dreamtime sack
Slung over
His shadowy shoulder.

Nocturnal

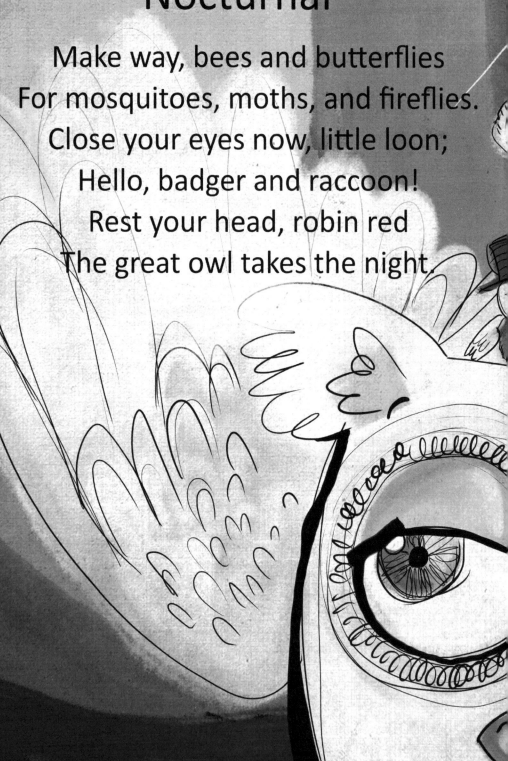

Make way, bees and butterflies
For mosquitoes, moths, and fireflies.
Close your eyes now, little loon;
Hello, badger and raccoon!
Rest your head, robin red
The great owl takes the night.

Hallow's Eve

Gone is summer's sun and heat,
Brown leaves rustle where they meet.

Brown leaves rustle where they meet,
The moon hangs stars for us to greet.

The moon hangs stars for us to greet,
Lights glow orange on the street.

Lights glow orange on the street,
A figure bobs beneath a sheet.

A figure bobs beneath a sheet,
The pitter patter of small feet.

The pitter patter of small feet,
Children out to trick or treat.

Train

By day a silver centipede
Chugging down the track,
By night the train's a bright-eyed snake
Nosing through the black;
The rattling, hissing front pulling
The long and slithery back.

Bat

Umbrella-webbed wings
Whipping the air;
Tossed to the sky,
Orbiting there.

The silver of moon
Glistens a bit
On the black on black,
On the flitter and flit.

A whisk through the night,
A shiver, a rush;
Then hung upside down
In an ebony hush.

The Fairy Ring

All night long
The elfin king
Lets his children
Play and sing.
The fairies laugh
And take to wing
Dancing round
The fairy ring.

I wish I could participate,
But Mom says
Bedtime
Is at eight!

Night Skating

On silver blades
I slice the ice,
Sketching,
Etching
The lake's smooth surface.
I am an artist,
This frozen water my canvas.

I'm pen on paper;

My feet ride the easel

Until the full moon appears,

And winking

Shines me a passage

I carve my signature on,

Skating all the way

Back home.

Christmas Eve

365 evenings
A year,
But only
This one

Winter's Night

Night is black
But winter white;
She decorates the dark in light
With tufts of snow,
And crystals bright.
Night is black
But winter
White.

If I were a Being from the Center of Earth

If I were a being
From the center of Earth
I'd come to the surface
At night.
I'd bear truth and knowledge
Of galaxies,
Of comet
And meteorite.
I'd offer the crystals
That come from the core,
The stones and the gems
Known in ancient folklore.
And, oh, to know all about
Our planet's birth
If I were a being
From the center of Earth!

5 P.M.

Whispering secrets
To anyone who'll listen,
The wind scrambles by.

5 A.M.

Sunflowers on guard
For the first ray of sunshine
Stand tall and patient.

Detective

Night
Clamors into corners,
Nestling
Into nooks and crannies.
My dog tucks his sleepy snout
Beneath a paw
And settles into a sphere.

Only the cat,
With moon-mirrored
Luminescent eyes
Dares to investigate.

Candle

The flame will flit,
The flame will flick,
Will dance and sway
And pull a trick
Of casting shadows
Tall and wide
Allowing dark
To creep behind
My chilling back
Until I find

...the light switch!

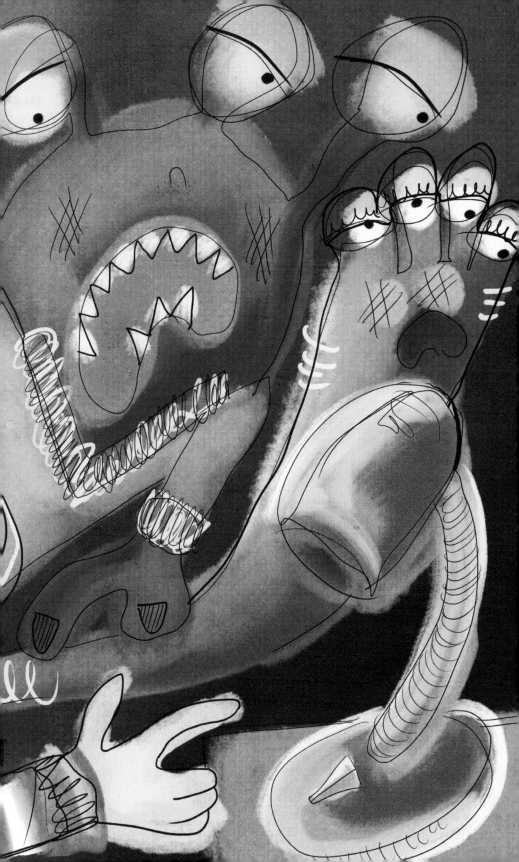

Evening in the City

Beehives of buildings
Where millions reside
Glow honey-yellow
When lit from inside.

There's a buzz,
A drone;
A taxi swarm beeps.
There's never a night
The big city sleeps.

Sleepover

Armed with blankets
And flashlights;
Sleepovers
On Friday nights.

Watch a movie,
Play charades;
Buttered bowls
Of popcorn made.

We pillow-fight,
Play truth or dare,
Tell ghost stories
'Til we're scared -

Then my brother
(As if on cue)
Bangs on our door
And yells out, "Boo!"

My Dream Catcher

Only sugarplum dreams
Come through
Its honeysuckle halo.

Nightmare snatcher,
My Dream Catcher.

Breakfast at Dawn

The skillet sky
Warms up
To a pale buttery yellow
As mists rise.
A crack! And a ray
Pierces the low-lying clouds,
Sizzling across the horizon,
And before you know it
Night's gone

Raven Howell

Award winning children's poet and picture book author Raven Howell has several published titles including Gibber/ Animal Acrostics and A Star Full of Sky. Her work is featured in the Parents' Choice award children's video, Noodlebug, and she's received three awards from the SCBWI. She writes poetry for children's magazines, and delights in presenting poetry workshops, visiting libraries and working in elementary classrooms.

Growing up in a household of poetry and song, Raven now lives with her husband in the Hudson Valley, enjoys time with her children, artwork, baking, a good mystery read, walking up and over mountains and across ocean beaches, sunshine and starry skies!

www.ravenhowell.com
https://www.facebook.com/raven.howell.75

Carina Povarchik

Born, raised and currently living in Argentina, Carina usually signs her works as Catru. Carina's parent's house was full of tools and handcrafted products made by them. That's where she got her love for creating.

Carina always did lots of things and tried all kinds of techniques. When 5 years old, she made paintings with ink using her own style and sold them on the street. Carina first graduated from a short computer program and then went on to graduate with a Bachelors in Educational Technologies. She subsequently taught computer programming at the college level, for many years. In 2007, she received, as a birthday surprise gift, a drawing tablet. And there, it all began.

catruillustration.com

CPSIA information can be obtained at www.ICGtesting.com
Printed in the USA
LVIW01n2313191117
556960LV00009B/32